## Team Spirit

# THE MILWAUKEE BREWERS

BY

MARK STEWART

Content Consultant
James L. Gates, Jr.
Library Director
National Baseball Hall of Fame and Museum

NORWOOD HOUSE PRESS
CHICAGO, ILLINOIS

Norwood House Press
P.O. Box 316598
Chicago, Illinois 60631

For information regarding Norwood House Press, please visit our website at:
www.norwoodhousepress.com or call 866-565-2900.

All photos courtesy of Getty Images except the following:
Black Book archives (7, 21 top); Topps, Inc. (14, 21 bottom, 34 bottom right, 36, 37,
40 top left, 41 top & bottom right, 43); Author's collection (34 bottom left);
BBCM (40 bottom left). Cover photo by Jonathan Daniel/Getty Images.
Special thanks to Topps, Inc.

Editor: Mike Kennedy
Designer: Ron Jaffe
Project Management: Black Book Partners, LLC.
Special thanks to Maris Associates and Tom Hurlburt.

Library of Congress Cataloging-in-Publication Data

Stewart, Mark, 1960-
  The Milwaukee Brewers / by Mark Stewart ; content consultant, James L.
Gates, Jr.
     p. cm. -- (Team spirit)
  Summary: "Presents the history, accomplishments and key personalities of
the Milwaukee Brewers baseball team. Includes timelines, quotes, maps,
glossary and websites"--Provided by publisher.
  Includes bibliographical references and index.
  ISBN-13: 978-1-59953-169-4 (library edition : alk. paper)
  ISBN-10: 1-59953-169-0 (library edition : alk. paper) 1. Milwaukee
Brewers (Baseball team)--History--Juvenile literature.  I. Gates, James L.
II. Title.
GV875.M53S84 2008
796.357'640977595--dc22
                                                        2007043500

**COVER PHOTO**: The Brewers celebrate a victory during the 2007 season.

# Table of Contents

SPORTS WORDS & VOCABULARY WORDS: In this book, you will find many words that are new to you. You may also see familiar words used in new ways. The glossary on page 46 gives the meanings of baseball words, as well as "everyday" words that have special baseball meanings. These words appear in **bold type** throughout the book. The glossary on page 47 gives the meanings of vocabulary words that are not related to baseball. They appear in ***bold italic type*** throughout the book.

# Meet the Brewers

One of the oldest beverages known to man is beer. It is brewed with hops, barley, and other grains. In ancient times, it provided important vitamins and nourishment. In the United States, the most famous beer-making city is Milwaukee, Wisconsin. What better name for a Milwaukee team than the Brewers?

The Brewers are *cherished* by their city. They play with great spirit on the field and get to know the fans off of it. In an era when many players change teams from year to year, the Brewers are known for keeping their players year after year.

This book tells the story of the Brewers. They work hard, and they work together. They are as close to a family as you will find in baseball. Even after a player leaves the team or retires, he knows that Milwaukee fans consider him a Brewer for life.

Geoff Jenkins, Bill Hall, and Corey Hart leap high in the air to celebrate a win during the 2007 season.

# Way Back When

When **Major League Baseball** searched for room to grow during the 1950s and 1960s, it looked to the west. In 1969, the **American League (AL)** added two new teams—one in Kansas City, Missouri and another in Seattle, Washington. The Seattle team was called the Pilots.

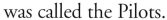

The Pilots had some good players, including Marty Pattin and Tommy Harper. However, they were not good enough to bring fans into creaky Sicks' Stadium, which was in need of repair. Just before the start of the 1970 season, Seattle's owners gave up on the team and sold it to a young automobile dealer named Bud Selig. He would later become commissioner of baseball.

Selig and his partners moved the team to Milwaukee. A club called the Braves had played there before moving to Atlanta a few years earlier. The fans in Milwaukee loved baseball and were thrilled to have another team. Even though the newly named Brewers lost 97 times, almost one million fans came to the ballpark to cheer for them.

The Brewers built an exciting team during the 1970s. They **drafted** and traded for young players who blossomed into great stars. Robin Yount, Paul Molitor, Darrell Porter, Gorman Thomas, Sixto Lezcano, Charlie Moore, and Jim Slaton all "grew up" together as Brewers. George Scott, Cecil Cooper, Ben Oglivie, Sal Bando, Don Money, Ted Simmons, and Mike Caldwell joined Milwaukee from other teams. Many of those players became **All-Stars**, and Yount and Molitor would later go into the **Hall of Fame**.

In 1982, the Brewers won the AL **pennant**. They were a hard-hitting bunch led by Molitor and Yount, and managed by Harvey Kuenn. The fans nicknamed them "Harvey's Wallbangers." Newcomers Pete Vuckovich, Rollie Fingers, and Don Sutton gave the Brewers great pitching. They met the St. Louis Cardinals in the **World Series** and lost in seven exciting games.

LEFT: Bug Selig poses with Don Sutton, who smiles as he shows off his Hall of Fame plaque.     **ABOVE**: Paul Molitor, one of the leaders of "Harvey's Wallbangers."

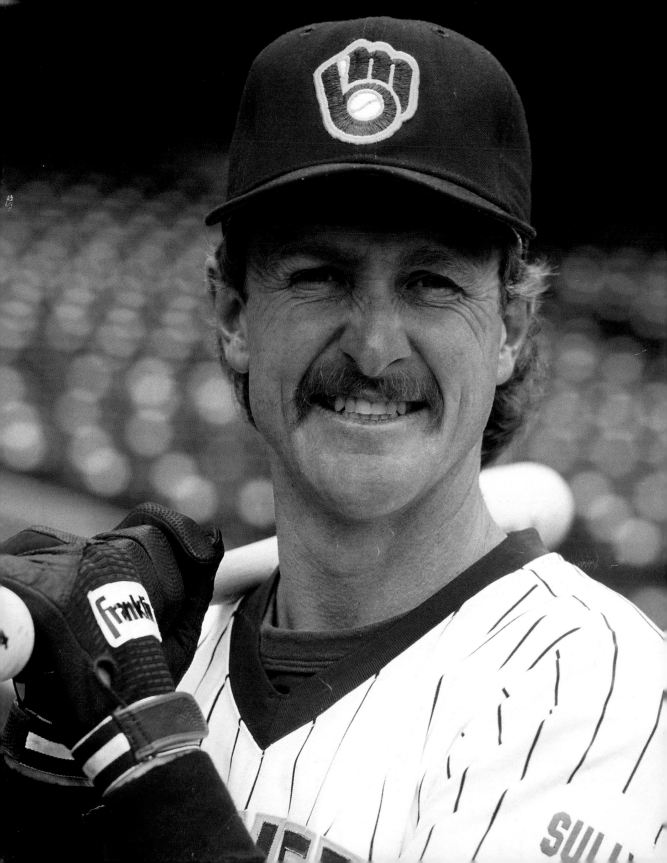

The Brewers went through some ups and downs in the 1980s and 1990s. They had always looked to their star players for leadership. After Molitor and Yount left the club, no one stepped up to fill their shoes. Teddy Higuera, Dan Plesac, Cal Eldred,

B.J. Surhoff, Greg Vaughn, Jeromy Burnitz, and Jeff Cirillo were all fine players, but they could not bring a pennant back to Milwaukee.

In 1998, the American League and **National League (NL)** voted to add one team each. That would make 30 teams in all, but 15 in each league. An even number is needed in each league so that every team always has an opponent to play. The Brewers agreed to move from the AL to the NL. It was the first time in the 20th *century* that a team had switched leagues. Milwaukee fans began the 21st century looking forward to new rivals, new opportunities, and a new *generation* of rising young stars.

**LEFT**: Robin Yount, the most popular player in Brewers history.
**ABOVE**: Teddy Higuera, Milwaukee's ace in the late 1980s.

# The Team Today

The Brewers look to their past to chart a course for their future. They had once built a pennant winner with young stars and *experienced* role players. Milwaukee's coaches let them play together and learn to trust one another. In the late 1990s, Milwaukee put that plan in motion again.

In 2007, the Brewers fought for the **NL Central** crown until the last week of the season. For much of the year, they were in first place. They had baseball's best young infield, including Prince Fielder, Rickie Weeks, J.J. Hardy, and Ryan Braun. Young pitchers Ben Sheets, Chris Capuano, and Yavani Gallardo gave the Brewers a chance to win every day.

With the support of talented players such as Bill Hall, Geoff Jenkins, Corey Hart, and Francisco Cordero, the Brewers *assembled* the building blocks they needed to compete every year. They know Milwaukee fans will be behind them every step of the way.

Ryan Braun is greeted by excited teammates Tony Gwynn Jr. and Rickie Weeks after scoring the winning run in a 2007 game.

# Home Turf

During the one season the team played as the Seattle Pilots, its stadium was the smallest in baseball. Sicks' Stadium held only 18,000 fans. This was one of the reasons the team moved to Milwaukee in 1970. For the next 31 seasons, the Brewers made their home in Milwaukee County Stadium. From 1953 to 1965, the Milwaukee Braves had played there.

In 2001, a magnificent new baseball stadium called Miller Park opened in Milwaukee. It combined old and new ***architecture*** in very creative ways. The stadium's ***retractable*** roof sweeps to two sides. The grass on the field was brought over from Milwaukee County Stadium.

## BY THE NUMBERS

- *There are 41,900 seats in the Brewers' stadium.*
- *The distance from home plate to the left field foul pole is 344 feet.*
- *The distance from home plate to the center field fence is 400 feet.*
- *The distance from home plate to the right field foul pole is 345 feet.*
- *The Brewers beat the Cincinnati Reds 5–4 in the first game played in Miller Park.*

On nice days, the Brewers keep the roof of their stadium open to let the sunshine in.

# Dressed for Success

The colors of the Seattle Pilots in 1969 were blue and gold. The team kept those colors a year later when it became the Brewers. Milwaukee wore white uniforms at home and light blue on the road. The team started using a two-tone hat in 1974.

In 1978, the Brewers switched to a home uniform with blue pinstripes. That year, they changed the lettering on their caps from a big *M* to the letters *m-b*, which made the shape of a glove and ball. Today, the Brewers wear several different uniforms, including versions that spell out either *Milwaukee* or *Brewers* in script across the front of the jersey.

In the Brewers' early years, the team's **logo** showed a batter shaped like a can. The team, however, does not encourage fans to drink alcohol. Rather, Milwaukee's name honors the people who have brewed beer there since the 1800s. Today, the logo includes a picture of the grains used to make this product.

Rollie Fingers models Milwaukee's pinstriped uniform of the 1980s.

The baseball uniform has not changed much since the Brewers began playing. It has four main parts:

- a cap or batting helmet with a sun visor
- a top with a player's number on the back
- pants that reach down between the ankle and the knee
- stirrup-style socks

The uniform top sometimes has a player's name on the back. The team's name, city, or logo is usually on the front. Baseball teams wear light-colored uniforms when they play at home and darker styles when they play on the road.

For more than 100 years, baseball uniforms were made of wool *flannel* and were very baggy. This helped the sweat *evaporate* and gave players the freedom to move around. Today's uniforms are made of *synthetic* fabrics that stretch with players and keep them dry and cool.

J.J. Hardy moves to field a ground ball in one of Milwaukee's 2007 home uniforms.

# We Won!

The story of the 1982 Brewers is one of the most amazing in baseball history. Milwaukee had spent years building a great young team, but the club started the season slowly. After 47 games, the Brewers were in fifth place in the **AL East** and going nowhere. The owner, Bud Selig, wanted to find a new manager. He asked Sal

Bando, a team *executive* and former Milwaukee star, to take the job, but Bando refused. Next Selig turned to Harvey Kuenn, his batting coach. Kuenn agreed to accept the challenge.

Kuenn had suffered through a series of illnesses, but each spring he was back in a Milwaukee uniform teaching the Brewers how to hit. The players loved him. Kuenn told them to relax and remember that baseball should be a fun game. The Brewers started smiling a little more—and hitting the ball *a lot* more. Soon they were being called "Harvey's Wallbangers."

Robin Yount, Paul Molitor, and Cecil Cooper found themselves in a three-way race for the most hits in the AL. Gorman Thomas and Ben Oglivie were among the league leaders in home runs. Pete Vuckovich and Mike Caldwell were winning almost every game they started, and Rollie Fingers was piling up **saves**. By the end of August, the Brewers had a big lead in the division over the Baltimore Orioles and Boston Red Sox.

The Brewers traded for former All-Star Don Sutton to have an experienced pitcher in September. They would need him, because Fingers hurt his

elbow and could not take the mound again. The Orioles and Brewers played in Baltimore on the final weekend, with just three games

**LEFT**: Brewers manager Harvey Kuenn.
**RIGHT**: Robin Yount takes a swing during the 1982 season.

separating the two teams. The Orioles won a **doubleheader** on Friday and won again on Saturday. The last game of the season would decide the division championship.

Sutton took the mound against another **veteran**, Jim Palmer. Yount, who would be named the league's **Most Valuable Player (MVP)** several weeks later, smashed two home runs to quiet the loud Baltimore crowd, and the Brewers went on to win 10–2.

In the **American League Championship Series (ALCS)**, the Brewers went right to the edge again. The California Angels won the first two games, but the Brewers roared back to win the final three. It was the team's first pennant. Milwaukee's luck finally ran out in the World Series against the St. Louis Cardinals. The Brewers led three games to two, but without Fingers, they could not hold off the talented Cardinals.

**ABOVE**: Don Sutton, who won several big games for the Brewers late in the 1982 season.    **RIGHT**: Mike Caldwell celebrates his victory in Game One of the 1982 World Series.

# Go-To Guys

To be a true star in baseball, you need more than a quick bat and a strong arm. You have to be a "go-to guy"—someone the manager wants on the pitcher's mound or in the batter's box when it matters most. Fans of the Brewers have had a lot to cheer about over the years, including these great stars …

## THE PIONEERS

### GEORGE SCOTT                                   First Baseman

• BORN: 3/23/1944   • PLAYED FOR TEAM: 1972 TO 1976

George Scott was a strong hitter and wonderful fielder. He tied for the AL home run crown in 1975 and won a **Gold Glove** every year he played for the Brewers.

### GORMAN THOMAS                                   Outfielder

• BORN: 12/12/1950

• PLAYED FOR TEAM: 1973 TO 1983 & 1986

Gorman Thomas was the first player picked by the Seattle Pilots in the 1969 baseball draft. He was known for crashing into outfield fences as a center fielder and slamming balls over them as a hitter. Thomas led the AL in home runs in 1979 and 1982.

**ABOVE**: Gorman Thomas
**TOP RIGHT**: Robin Yount     **BOTTOM RIGHT**: Cecil Cooper

## ROBIN YOUNT — Shortstop/Outfielder

- BORN: 9/16/1955   • PLAYED FOR TEAM: 1974 TO 1993

Most fans believe that Robin Yount was the greatest of all Brewers. In 1982, he led the team to the pennant and was named AL MVP. Yount captured the award again in 1989. He had 3,142 hits in his career.

## JIM GANTNER — Second Baseman/Third Baseman

- BORN: 1/5/1953   • PLAYED FOR TEAM: 1976 TO 1992

Jim Gantner did whatever the Brewers needed at bat or in the field. He was beloved by his teammates and by the Milwaukee fans.

## CECIL COOPER — First Baseman

- BORN: 12/20/1949   • PLAYED FOR TEAM: 1977 TO 1987

Cecil Cooper was a smooth fielder and a great hitter. He batted over .300 season after season and led the AL in **runs batted in (RBI)** in 1980 and 1983. In 1982, Cooper got the hit that won the pennant for Milwaukee.

## PAUL MOLITOR — Second Baseman/ Third Baseman/Designated Hitter

- BORN: 8/22/1956   • PLAYED FOR TEAM: 1978 TO 1992

Paul Molitor was one of the finest hitters and baserunners in history. He led the AL in runs scored three times for the Brewers and had a 39-game hitting streak in 1987. Molitor was a **versatile** star who played the infield and outfield for Milwaukee.

# MODERN STARS

## GREG VAUGHN                                    Outfielder

• BORN: 7/3/1965    • PLAYED FOR TEAM: 1989 TO 1996

Greg Vaughn was one of the most powerful hitters in baseball. He led the Brewers in home runs four years in a row.

## JEFF CIRILLO                                  Third Baseman

• BORN: 9/23/1969   • PLAYED FOR TEAM: 1994 TO 1999 & 2005 TO 2006

The Brewers believed Jeff Cirillo was best suited to be a utility player—until he hit his way into their everyday **lineup**. He batted .300 or better almost every year after that.

## BEN SHEETS    Pitcher

• BORN: 7/18/1978

• FIRST YEAR WITH TEAM: 2001

Ben Sheets arrived in the majors with three great pitches—a fastball, curve, and **changeup**. He used all of them to set a team record for strikeouts in 2004.

**ABOVE**: Ben Sheets
**TOP RIGHT**: J.J. Hardy    **BOTTOM RIGHT**: Ryan Braun and Prince Fielder

## J.J. HARDY    Shortstop

- BORN: 8/19/1982
- FIRST YEAR WITH TEAM: 2005

The Brewers drafted J.J. Hardy because of his hitting. When he made it to the majors, he showed he was a great fielder, too.

## PRINCE FIELDER    First Baseman

- BORN: 5/9/1984
- FIRST YEAR WITH TEAM: 2005

Prince Fielder's father, Cecil, was a home run champion for the Detroit Tigers. In 2007, Prince followed in his dad's footsteps by leading the NL with 50 homers.

## RYAN BRAUN    Third Baseman

- BORN: 11/17/1983    • FIRST YEAR WITH TEAM: 2007

Ryan Braun had one of the greatest years ever by a Milwaukee **rookie** in 2007. In less than a full season, he batted .324 with 34 home runs and 97 runs batted in. Braun was the final piece of the Brewers' exciting young infield.

# On the Sidelines

The Brewers had some good managers in their early years, including Dave Bristol, Del Crandall, George Bamberger, and Buck Rodgers. The hitting coach for all of those managers was Harvey Kuenn. He was a former batting champion who had survived open-heart surgery, kidney failure, and a leg amputation. Kuenn cherished life, and after he was named manager in 1982, he told his players to do the same. A few months later, they were AL champions!

In the years that followed, Tom Trebelhorn, Phil Garner, and Davey Lopes managed the Brewers. They did well with the talent they had, but Milwaukee never seemed to put together all the right pieces. Most years, the team dropped out of the pennant race by summer.

In 2003, Ned Yost took over as manager of the Brewers. He had been a coach under Bobby Cox for many years with the Atlanta Braves. From Cox, Yost learned how to get the most out of his players. He used those lessons to turn the Brewers into pennant contenders in 2007.

Brewers manager Ned Yost poses for a picture with Milwaukee's beloved announcer Bob Uecker.

# One Great Day

After losing the first two games of the 1982 American League Championship Series, the Brewers had a long plane ride home from California. All the way, they thought about how the Angels had beaten them twice. One more defeat and Milwaukee would be **eliminated** from the **playoffs**.

The Brewers refused to lose at home. Don Sutton won Game Three, and Moose Haas pitched Milwaukee to another victory in Game Four. The series was now even. Game Five would decide the pennant.

Milwaukee manager Harvey Kuenn sent Pete Vuckovich to the mound in front of a packed house at Milwaukee County Stadium. Vuckovich struggled early on. He gave up three runs in the first four innings, and the Brewers trailed 3–1.

LEFT: Moose Haas, who won Game Four to even the series against the California Angels.
RIGHT: Milwaukee slugger Ben Oglivie.

Milwaukee was down but not out. Ben Oglivie hit a home run to cut California's lead to 3–2. That was the score when the Brewers came to bat in the bottom of the seventh inning. Charlie Moore, Jim Gantner, and Robin Yount got on base. Then Cecil Cooper stepped into the batter's box with two outs. He guided a pitch by Luis Sanchez into left field for a single. Moore and Gantner raced home to give the Brewers a 4–3 lead.

The Angels put a man on base in the ninth inning. Normally, the Brewers turned to Rollie Fingers in those situations. But their star **relief pitcher** was hurt and unavailable. Kuenn turned instead to Pete Ladd, a big rookie who had thrown just 18 innings that season. With the crowd buzzing with excitement, Ladd came into the game and calmly got the final three outs. The players ran out of the dugout and the fans poured onto the field to celebrate with the new AL champions.

27

# Legend Has It

## Who was the first Bernie Brewer?

**LEGEND HAS IT** that Milt Mason was. Bernie Brewer is the Milwaukee *mascot*. In the team's first season, Mason climbed to the top of the scoreboard on July 6th and announced that he would not come down until a crowd of 40,000 came to a Brewers game. He was up there until August! A few years later, the Brewers decided to put someone high above the outfield as their mascot. Bernie Brewer now has a much fancier home than Mason did.

**ABOVE**: Milwaukee mascot Bernie Brewer.

# Why was Henry Aaron annoyed after the final hit of his career?

**LEGEND HAS IT** that he wanted to score one last run. On the final day of the 1976 season, Aaron—who finished his career with the Brewers—hit a ball into the outfield and stopped at first base for his 3,771st hit. He was surprised to see **pinch-runner** Jim Gantner come out of the Brewers' dugout to replace him. The manager wanted Aaron to get one last *ovation* as he walked off the field. When Aaron returned to the dugout he was frowning—had he scored one more run he would have passed Babe Ruth on the all-time list.

# Who was Milwaukee's biggest hot dog?

**LEGEND HAS IT** that Javon Walker was. The former Green Bay Packers football star once squeezed into a seven-foot foam costume and competed in the Brewers' popular Sausage Race. The race is held at the bottom of the sixth inning between different types of "wieners," including a Polish sausage, bratwurst, chorizo, and hot dog. Walker raced as an Italian sausage.

# It Really Happened

The 1987 season was the "streakiest" ever for the Brewers—and maybe for any team in baseball history. They began the year by beating the Boston Red Sox 5–1 in Milwaukee on Opening Day. The Brewers went on to win the next two and sweep the three-game series. Next they traveled to Texas, where they won three in a row from the Rangers.

The 6–0 Brewers flew to Baltimore to play the Orioles. They won three more games, including a **no-hitter** by Juan Nieves. It was the first in team history. The Brewers returned to Milwaukee and won three games to go 12–0. A few days later in Chicago, they defeated the White Sox to set an AL record for the best start to a season. The team finally lost on April 21st.

There were more streaks that season. From May 3rd to May 19th, the Brewers lost 12 games in a row. After the All-Star break, Paul Molitor launched an amazing hitting streak. He got at least one hit in 39 games in a row. Teddy Higuera, the team's best pitcher, also joined in the fun. During one stretch, he threw three **shutouts** in a row and set a team record with 32 straight scoreless innings.

Paul Molitor, who thrilled fans in 1987 with his 39-game hitting streak.

# Team Spirit

There are few places in baseball that are more fun than a Brewers game. At the stadium, the food is good, the prices are low, and the views are excellent. The **bleacher seats** in the outfield are a favorite of fans from nearby colleges. They cheer loudest in the sixth inning, when the Sausage Race is held.

A bond shared by all Milwaukee fans is their love of Bob Uecker, who became the voice of the Brewers in 1970. He is one of the funniest people in baseball. Whenever there is a break in the action, "Ueck" fills the time with hilarious stories about baseball in the 1950s and 1960s. For many years, he was a catcher—though not a very good one, he admits.

Whenever a Brewer hits a home run, the fans listen for Uecker's famous call: "Get up … Get up … Get outta here … Gone!" Milwaukee home runs also mean it is time for Bernie Brewer to take a trip down his slide in left field. He also goes into action at the end of a Milwaukee victory.

Every day is a "race day" at a Brewers game.

# Timeline

George
Scott

**1970**
The team moves to
Milwaukee and is
renamed the Brewers.

**1976**
George Scott wins his fifth Gold
Glove in a row for the Brewers.

**1969**
The team plays its
first season as the
Seattle Pilots.

**1978**
The team has its first
winning season.

**1982**
The Brewers win
the AL pennant.

A Seattle Pilots
souvenir patch

Don Money, a
key member of the
1982 AL champs.

DON MONEY

Robin
Yount

Jeff Cirillo and
Jeromy Burnitz
slap a high
five during the
1998 season.

**1989**
Robin Yount wins his
second MVP award.

**1998**
The Brewers switch
from the AL to the NL.

**2001**
Miller Park opens
in Milwaukee.

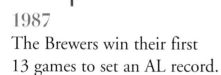

**1987**
The Brewers win their first
13 games to set an AL record.

**1992**
Pat Listach is named
**Rookie of the Year**.

**2007**
Prince Fielder sets
a team record with
50 home runs.

Pat
Listach

Prince
Fielder

# Fun Facts

## MAN OF STEAL

The only Seattle Pilot to lead the majors in a major statistic was Tommy Harper. He stole 73 bases in 1969.

## YOUNG PRINCE

Prince Fielder was hitting home runs years before he became a Brewer. When he was 12, he took batting practice with his father's team, the Detroit Tigers. The players were amazed when he smashed a ball into the seats.

## LUCKY 13

In 1969, Gene Brabender won 13 games for the Seattle Pilots. It was the most wins ever by a pitcher for an **expansion team**.

## DOWN UNDER WONDERS

In 1993, Milwaukee's Graeme Lloyd and Dave Nilsson became baseball's first Australian pitcher-catcher combination.

**ABOVE**: Tommy Harper
**RIGHT**: Henry "Hank" Aaron

## TROPHY CASE

Ryan Braun was named NL Player of the Month and NL Rookie of the Month in July 2007. No one had ever won both awards in the same month.

## MILWAUKEE CONNECTION

Only two players wore the uniform of the Milwaukee Braves and Milwaukee Brewers—Henry Aaron and Phil Roof.

## WHAT A RELIEF

In 1998, Milwaukee had a very busy **bullpen**. The Brewers used relievers in 160 of their 162 games.

## ZEROED IN

In 1971, the Brewers pitched 23 shutouts. Marty Pattin led the team with five. Fans had an exciting season—60 of Milwaukee's games were won or lost by just one run!

# Talking Baseball

"To have guys like this not only as teammates, but as friends made it where I couldn't wait to go to the ballpark every day."
—*Robin Yount, on the Milwaukee clubhouse in the 1970s and 1980s*

"He's one of the finest gentlemen I've ever known. I loved having him as a player."
—*Bud Selig, on team leader Cecil Cooper*

"I'd like to stay with the Brewers for my whole career, just like Robin Yount. That's what I'd like to do. That would be something special."
—*J.J. Hardy, on his future with the team*

"I love interacting with people and doing pretty much anything with people."
—*Ryan Braun, on his friendships with the fans*

"They said I was such a great prospect that they were sending me to a winter league to sharpen up. When I stepped off the plane, I was in Greenland!"

*—Bob Uecker, joking about his career as a player*

"If there's a man on second, I'm trying to get him in with a base hit. The doubles and homers will come."

*—Prince Fielder, on hitting for the situation and not for the stats*

"Everyone else was growing regular moustaches and I thought I'd do it different, so I let it grow and put wax on it and it's been with me ever since."

*—Rollie Fingers, on his famous handlebar moustache*

"Baseball is a really strange game. It will humble you in a heartbeat … It has its ways of testing you."

*—Ned Yost, on the challenges of managing*

"If I knew exactly what I know now and had it to do over, I'd be a **switch-hitter**. No telling what I could have done."

*—Henry Aaron, on hitting all of his 755 home runs right-handed*

**LEFT**: Ryan Braun and J.J. Hardy     **ABOVE**: Rollie Fingers

# For the Record

The great Brewers teams and players have left their marks on the record books. These are the "best of the best" …

Robin Yount

## BREWERS AWARD WINNERS

| WINNER | AWARD | YEAR |
|---|---|---|
| Mike Caldwell | Comeback Player of the Year | 1978 |
| George Bamberger | Manager of the Year | 1978 |
| Rollie Fingers | Cy Young Award* | 1981 |
| Rollie Fingers | Most Valuable Player | 1981 |
| Pete Vuckovich | Cy Young Award | 1982 |
| Robin Yount | Most Valuable Player | 1982 |
| Harvey Kuenn | Manager of the Year | 1982 |
| Robin Yount | Most Valuable Player | 1989 |
| Pat Listach | Rookie of the Year | 1992 |
| Ryan Braun | Rookie of the Year | 2007 |

* The annual trophy given to each league's best pitcher.

Pat Listach

Ryan Braun

## BREWERS ACHIEVEMENTS

| ACHIEVEMENT | YEAR |
| --- | --- |
| AL East Second-Half Champions* | 1981 |
| AL East Champions | 1982 |
| AL Pennant Winners | 1982 |

*The 1981 season was split into two halves because of a labor dispute.*

PITCHER **MIKE CALDWELL**
BREWERS

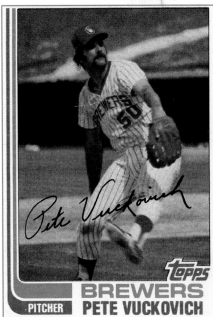

PITCHER **PETE VUCKOVICH**
BREWERS

Ted Simmons (**LEFT**), Mike Caldwell (**TOP**), and Pete Vuckovich (**ABOVE**), key players on the 1982 team.

# Pinpoints

The history of a baseball team is made up of many smaller stories. These stories take place all over the map—not just in the city a team calls "home." Match the pushpins on these maps to the Team Facts and you will begin to see the story of the Brewers unfold!

# TEAM FACTS

**1** Milwaukee, Wisconsin—*The Brewers have played here since 1970.*

**2** Danville, Illinois—*Robin Yount was born here.*

**3** St. Paul, Minnesota—*Paul Molitor was born here.*

**4** Seattle, Washington—*The team played one season here as the Pilots in 1969.*

**5** Brenham, Texas—*Cecil Cooper was born here.*

**6** Johnstown, Pennsylvania—*Pete Vuckovich was born here.*

**7** Charleston, South Carolina—*Gorman Thomas was born here.*

**8** Baton Rouge, Louisiana—*Ben Sheets was born here.*

**9** Nettleton, Mississippi—*Bill Hall was born here.*

**10** Brisbane, Australia—*Dave Nilsson was born here.*

**11** Los Mochis, Mexico—*Teddy Higuera was born here.*

**12** Arecibo, Puerto Rico—*Sixto Lezcano was born here.*

Paul Molitor

# Play Ball

Baseball is a game played between two teams over nine innings. Teams take one turn at bat and one turn in the field during each inning. A turn at bat ends when three outs are made. The batters on the hitting team try to reach base safely. The players on the fielding team try to prevent this from happening.

In baseball, the ball is controlled by the pitcher. The pitcher must throw the ball to the batter, who decides whether or not to swing at each pitch. If a batter swings and misses, it is a strike. If the batter lets a good pitch go by, it is also a strike. If the batter swings and the ball does not stay in fair territory (between the v-shaped lines that begin at home plate) it is called "foul," and is counted as a strike. If the pitcher throws three strikes, the batter is out. If the pitcher throws four bad pitches before that, the batter is awarded first base. This is called a base-on-balls, or "walk."

When the batter swings the bat and hits the ball, everyone springs into action. If a fielder catches a batted ball before it hits the ground, the batter is out. If a fielder scoops the ball off the ground and throws it to first base before the batter arrives, the batter is out. If the batter reaches first base safely, he is credited with a hit. A one-base hit is called a single, a two-base hit is called a double, a three-base hit is called a triple, and a four-base hit is called a home run.

Runners who reach base are only safe when they are touching one of the bases. If they are caught between the bases, the fielders can tag them with the ball and record an out.

A batter who is able to circle the bases and make it back to home plate before three outs are made is credited with a run scored. The team with the most runs after nine innings is the winner.

Anyone who has played baseball (or softball) knows that it can be a complicated game. Every player on the field has a job to do. Different players have different strengths and weaknesses. The pitchers, batters, and managers make hundreds of decisions every game. The more you play and watch baseball, the more "little things" you are likely to notice. The next time you are at a game, look for these plays:

## PLAY LIST

**DOUBLE PLAY**—A play where the fielding team is able to make two outs on one batted ball. This usually happens when a runner is on first base, and the batter hits a ground ball to one of the infielders. The base runner is forced out at second base and the ball is then thrown to first base before the batter arrives.

**HIT AND RUN**—A play where the runner on first base sprints to second base while the pitcher is throwing the ball to the batter. When the second baseman or shortstop moves toward the base to wait for the catcher's throw, the batter tries to hit the ball to the place that the fielder has just left. If the batter swings and misses, the fielding team can tag the runner out.

**INTENTIONAL WALK**—A play when the pitcher throws four bad pitches on purpose, allowing the batter to walk to first base. This happens when the pitcher would much rather face the next batter—and is willing to risk putting a runner on base.

**SACRIFICE BUNT**—A play where the batter makes an out on purpose so that a teammate can move to the next base. On a bunt, the batter tries to "deaden" the pitch with the bat instead of swinging at it.

**SHOESTRING CATCH**—A play where an outfielder catches a short hit an inch or two above the ground, near the tops of his shoes. It is not easy to run as fast as you can and lower your glove without slowing down. It can be risky, too. If a fielder misses a shoestring catch, the ball might roll all the way to the fence.

# Glossary

**AL EAST**—A group of American League teams that play in the eastern part of the country.

**ALL-STARS**—Players who are selected to play in baseball's annual All-Star Game.

**AMERICAN LEAGUE (AL)**—One of baseball's two major leagues; the AL began play in 1901.

**AMERICAN LEAGUE CHAMPIONSHIP SERIES (ALCS)**—The competition that has decided the AL pennant since 1969.

**BLEACHER SEATS**—The unprotected seats located in the outfield, where fans get "bleached" by the sun.

**BULLPEN**—The area where a team's relief pitchers warm up; this word also describes the group of relief pitchers in this area.

**CHANGEUP**—A slow pitch disguised to look like a fastball.

**DOUBLEHEADER**—Two games scheduled to be played in one day.

**DRAFTED**—Selected during the annual meeting at which teams take turns choosing the best players in high school and college.

**EXPANSION TEAM**—A new team added to a league.

**GOLD GLOVE**—An award given each year to baseball's best fielders.

**HALL OF FAME**—The museum in Cooperstown, New York, where baseball's greatest players are honored. A player voted into the Hall of Fame is sometimes called a "Hall of Famer."

**LINEUP**—The list of players who are playing in a game.

**MAJOR LEAGUE BASEBALL**—The top level of professional baseball leagues. The AL and NL make up today's major leagues. Sometimes called the "big leagues."

**MOST VALUABLE PLAYER (MVP)**—An award given each year to each league's top player; an MVP is also selected for the World Series and All-Star Game.

**NATIONAL LEAGUE (NL)**—The older of the two major leagues; the NL began play in 1876.

**NL CENTRAL**—A group of National League teams that plays in the central part of the country.

**NO-HITTER**—A game in which a team is unable to get a hit.

**PENNANT**—A league championship. The term comes from the triangular flag awarded to each season's champion, beginning in the 1870s.

**PINCH-RUNNER**—A player who is sent into the game to run for a teammate.

**PLAYOFFS**—The games played after the regular season to determine which teams will advance to the World Series.

**RELIEF PITCHER**—A pitcher who is brought into a game to replace another pitcher. Relief pitchers can be seen warming up in the bullpen.

**ROOKIE**—A player in his first season.

**ROOKIE OF THE YEAR**—An annual award given to each league's best first-year player.

**RUNS BATTED IN (RBI)**—A statistic that counts the number of runners a batter drives home.

**SAVES**—A statistic that counts the number of times a relief pitcher finishes off a close victory for his team.

**SHUTOUTS**—Games in which one team does not allow its opponent to score a run.

**SWITCH-HITTER**—A player who can hit from either side of home plate. Switch-hitters bat left-handed against right-handed pitchers, and right-handed against left-handed pitchers.

**VETERAN**—A player with many years of experience.

**WORLD SERIES**—The world championship series played between the winners of the NL and AL.

## OTHER WORDS TO KNOW

**ARCHITECTURE**—A style of building.

**ASSEMBLED**—Put together.

**CENTURY**—A period of 100 years.

**CHERISHED**—Showed great love for.

**ELIMINATED**—Gotten rid of.

**EVAPORATE**—Disappear, or turn into vapor.

**EXECUTIVE**—Someone who helps run a business.

**EXPERIENCED**—Having knowledge and skill in a job.

**FLANNEL**—A soft wool or cotton material.

**GENERATION**—A period of years roughly equal to the time it takes for a person to be born, grow up, and have children.

**LOGO**—A symbol or design that represents a company or team.

**MASCOT**—An animal or person believed to bring a group good luck.

**OVATION**—A long, loud cheer.

**RETRACTABLE**—Able to pull back.

**SYNTHETIC**—Made in a laboratory, not in nature.

**VERSATILE**—Able to do many things well.

# Places to Go

## ON THE ROAD

**MILWAUKEE BREWERS**
One Brewers Way
Milwaukee, Wisconsin 53214
(414) 902-4100

**NATIONAL BASEBALL HALL OF FAME AND MUSEUM**
25 Main Street
Cooperstown, New York 13326
(888) 425-5633
www.baseballhalloffame.org

## ON THE WEB

**THE MILWAUKEE BREWERS**
  • *Learn more about the Brewers*

www.milwaukeebrewers.com

**MAJOR LEAGUE BASEBALL**
  • *Learn more about all the major league teams*

www.mlb.com

**MINOR LEAGUE BASEBALL**
  • *Learn more about the minor leagues*

www.minorleaguebaseball.com

## ON THE BOOKSHELF

To learn more about the sport of baseball, look for these books at your library or bookstore:

• Kelly, James. *Baseball*. New York, New York: DK, 2005.

• Jacobs, Greg. *The Everything Kids' Baseball Book*. Cincinnati, Ohio: Adams Media Corporation, 2006.

• Stewart, Mark and Kennedy, Mike. *Long Ball: The Legend and Lore of the Home Run*. Minneapolis, Minnesota: Millbrook Press, 2006.

# Index

## The Team

**MARK STEWART** has written more than 25 books on baseball, and over 100 sports books for kids. He grew up in New York City during the 1960s rooting for the Yankees and Mets, and now takes his two daughters, Mariah and Rachel, to the same ball-parks. Mark comes from a family of writers. His grand-father was Sunday Editor of the *New York Times* and his mother was Articles Editor of *Ladies' Home Journal* and *McCall's*. Mark has profiled hundreds of athletes over the last 20 years. He has also written several books about his native New York and New Jersey, his home today. Mark is a graduate of Duke University, with a degree in history. He lives with his daughters and wife, Sarah, overlooking Sandy Hook, NJ.

**JAMES L. GATES, JR.** has served as Library Director at the National Baseball Hall of Fame since 1995. He had previously served in academic libraries for almost fifteen years. He holds degrees from Belmont Abbey College, the University of Notre Dame, and Indiana University. During his career Jim has authored several academic articles and has served in an editorial capacity on multiple book, magazine, and museum publications, and he also serves as host for the Annual Cooperstown Symposium on Baseball and American Culture. He is an ardent Baltimore Orioles fan and enjoys watching baseball with his wife and two children.